Christmas
and how to survive it

'Frankly, I'll be glad when it's all over.'

Christmas
and how to survive it

Joseph Connolly

with illustrations by Gray Jolliffe

Little Books by Big Names™

First published in the United Kingdom in 2003 by Little Books Ltd,
48 Catherine Place, London SW1E 6HL

10 9 8 7 6 5 4 3 2 1

A CIP catalogue record for this book is available from the British Library.

ISBN: 1 904435 05 X

The author and publisher will be grateful for any information that will
assist them in keeping future editions up-to-date. Although all reasonable care
has been taken in the preparation of this book, neither the publisher, editors nor
the author can accept any liability for any consequences arising from the use
thereof, or the information contained therein.

*Many thanks to: Jamie Ambrose for editorial management and design input,
Gray Jolliffe for illustrations, Ian Hughes at Mousemat Design for jacket
and text design, Margaret Campbell of Scan-Hi Digital and Craig
Campbell of QSP Print for printing consultancy.*

Printed and bound in Scotland by Scotprint.

contents

'I so did **NOT** want a pony!'

To Patricia, Victoria and Charles,
with love from Scrooge

the very first
stirrings of unease

Where and when does the lurking rumour of another Christmas looming first leap out and mug you? Your local department store will often have a great deal to do with it. Outside it is a scorcher (has been for days), and so you relish the store's fat hit of frozen air as you flit from floor to floor in quest of not just shorts and flip-flops, but also a desk-top fan.

But what do you see? Not just rack upon rack of thick and sensible winter coats; they are not even content to offend your sight with a larky pyramid of multicoloured scarf 'n' mitt sets (with optional and toning pom-pom lunatic's hat). No, no. For you are about to turn an inadvertent corner. You are

'Baa! Humbug!'

about to be momentarily confused. Because you are sure (you could swear to it) that here is where all the barbecue stuff is, isn't it?

No. It isn't.

Because what you see are...

Baubles.

Baubles, yes. And fir trees. And ranked-up masses of cellophane-trussed and gleaming bumper packs of *cards*. Not just advent calendars but fully-fledged, twelve-month calendars, each one bearing not just kittens or the leering faces of an assortment of transient and seemingly unsavoury idiots, but also a year that is utterly *alien* to your eye.

It is now. This is the moment when *the very first stirrings of unease* (which have been alive and well now for tens of minutes, eating away at the wall of your stomach) suddenly rally together and force you to face the fact that what you can no longer deny feeling is… sick.

Sick, yes – and quite angry, too. Why are these money-grabbing marketeers setting out their stall so goddamed *early*? Why are they robbing us of all this *summer*? How can they fail to respect the nature of *seasons*? And at this point, we must brace ourselves. We simply must do *the sensible thing*.

Which is: you go home. And (for now) you are going to forget it. Put it out of your mind. I'll tell you when to resurrect it (at the end of this section, as a matter of fact). But not yet. Forget it. See? You have done *the sensible thing*.

But. Some of you – at the first (or maybe the second) sight of those cheekily winking baubles – will be compelled and, without your remotely understanding as to *why*, exactly, will be swamped and hurtled into doing the wholly *unsensible* thing, and this is to PANIC.

Panic does have a way of getting hold of people. As, indeed, those who decide to lay out the Christmas departments in late summer will happily tell you, it is meant to do. You must resist it. Otherwise, you will become one of those people who seem to exist solely to drive the rest of us crazy: the people who attend to everything stupidly early.

And do not think that they are content to commence in September, these people. No, no. The previous January sale will have drawn them back to the battered and lacklustre remains of those self-same Christmas departments, where they crunch their way across the war-torn carpets of shattered pretty things and drifts of abandoned glitter and they will buy CHEAP from the shop assistants (these poor devils now glassy-eyed and near-deranged as they struggle to come to terms with being back behind these same sodding counters after that all-too-brief respite).

WELL, WHAT?

What will they buy, these undaunted souls? They will buy more cards – yes, more – and a further advent calendar and a fairy and maybe a five-foot artificial blue Scots pine (with cones attached).

FOR NEXT TIME.

So, come September, they are really doing no more than adding the finishing touches. And these people who do this – what do they make us? I'll tell you:

THEY MAKE US SICK.

And in no time they will tell you (and they always tell you, make no mistake: this is most of the point) that they have also chosen and purchased a variety of tasteful gifts for both friends and family. And they have not just *wrapped* them. Oh, no. They have wrapped them *beautifully*.

And shelved them neatly in a lofty cupboard set aside for just this purpose. And now, they will giddily assure you, they can relax. For about three months. Tinker, maybe, with just the odd all-but-foolproof, tried-and-tested recipe. Otherwise – all done. *All done.* You see? And at this point you experience a twinge of something else. It is *grudging*, admittedly, but it remains nonetheless clearly identifiable as *envy*.

Pure and simple (if envy can ever be either thing). And a gentle lick of panic is felt and even heard to squeak within you. Ignore it. You must now *hold your nerve.*

Sound advice. But be vigilant – because I'll tell you what could do for you now: the casual discovery of the first of many...

Guilt-inducing countdowns. There it lies. In black and white. An unabashed listing, by some hungover hack or other in a magazine that you'd think would know better, of all those things that by now you should have attended to, as well as all sorts of other things that would frankly not even so much as glance across a sane person's mind... all of which must really be seen to soon. Listen:

HOLD YOUR NERVE

Just keep repeating to yourself what is, after all, no more than the truth – there is plenty of time. Look out of the window: the sun is *shining*, for God's sake. It is still warmish. The roses have yet to blow out (and so have you). There is plenty of time. So relax. Try not to succumb to rebellion.

Why, you might think, should I do this at all? Hey? It's not as if it's *appreciated*, or anything (just look at last year: nearly bloody killed myself. Did I even get so much as a word of thanks? Did I buggery). So. Maybe we could go away this year.

Well, why not? Just log on for extra time off work (Christ knows I've earned it) and, you know – just take *off*. Go. Simply shoot away. Let someone else do all the work for a change. You might even go so far as getting hold of a brochure. One in which young, brown people loll on hammocks and toy with gaudy drinks. But then eventually, however, *these* will kick in:

RESPONSIBILITIES

The children. A traditional Christmas at home. The way we always do it. The cat. Husband: knackered, come December – deserves a rest. (Wives and mothers form no part of such musings; husbands and children simply don't *think* like this). And then there are the oldies to consider. And not least, of course, there is, um… well, not to put too fine a point on it… money.

Have you *seen* what these places are charging? I mean – good God! For that sort of money, I could order a sofa now (right this minute) at an unrepeatable price and be assured of guaranteed delivery in good time for… Christmas. Face it. It's maybe time to give in. The true countdown (the sane one) starts right here and now. But one more word about your nerve. It may be weakening, but it must not break.

SO. LET'S GO.

But first: a quick questionnaire to see if you've been drinking it all in.

QUESTIONNAIRE

1 What do you do when you see baubles for sale in: (a) September (b) October (c) November (d) December (e) January?

2 What do you do when someone tells you brightly in October that they have already seen to absolutely *everything*?

3 What do you do on sighting the very first guilt-inducing countdown in a magazine or newspaper?

4 What do you do if suddenly assailed by the urge to Go Away This Year?

'I hate flash photographs. They always make my eyes look red.'

ANSWERS:

1 (a) Feel sick. (b) Smirk. (c) Hold your nerve. (d) Succumb, queue endlessly to pay, and regret that they've run out of those pretty pink metallic spirals that they had loads of back in September. (e) Feel sick.

2 You tell yourself that they need to get a life. And then you silently wonder why in hell it is that you can't be a bit more *organized*.

3 You marvel at the fact that anyone could actually pay this hack to churn out the same old balls as last year. (God, how desperate can they be to fill up the pages?) And then you read it.

4 Get real. You're not going to – and that's that, quite frankly.

So: Christmas. Are you sitting comfortably? No? Well, for God's sake get yourself *sorted*, can't you?! (Sorry, but you'll need a firm hand as time goes by.)

Ready?

Good.

Now we can begin.

1

advent is now

It would be nice if I could tell you that Christmas comes in many guises, their diversity and abundance a joy to behold. Not remotely true. The basic breakdown is as follows. Are you:

(a) Single? (b) Not?

I say 'not' as opposed to 'married' because what we have to deal with here is really a question of *encumbrance*. Are you or are you not as free as a festive robin to flit about at will, hither and yon? No, I thought not. You see, if you are truly young (student, say) it is likely that you still live with your parents: hence encumbered. And even if you are sharing digs, ask yourself this: what will your flatmates all be doing, come Christmas? Exactly – going home to their parents. And so, therefore, will you.

Or maybe you find yourself, at this oh-so-special time, basking and purring in the first flush of true love.

Well then it's simple. On at least one of the days, you'll end up with theirs, or they'll end up with yours – it's the nature of the thing. Do not fall out over this. It's not worth it. Simply dwell upon the fornication to come, when all the socializing is done with. Meanwhile, try to single out the family boasting the largest house and the better cook, promising earnestly a total reversal *next* year – by which time, who knows, you might very well be basking and purring in the very first flush of true love with someone else entirely.

Maybe, however, you are divorced

This makes it worse (as if you needed to be told). What with one ex-family and the other ex-family, the mutual friends and cartloads of in-laws you won't have a moment to yourself. The key here, I'm afraid, is to go with the flow. Even if it kills you. Here's what you do:

1 Buy token gifts for all those you care for.
2 Buy token gifts for all those you'd rather not.
3 Buy token gifts for all those you quite frankly loathe.

And that's you, anyway, largely off the hook. Smile a good deal (alcohol will assist you. But of course. Alcohol is often seen as the essential oil that ensures that the wheels and cogs of Christmas do not seize up altogether). And if anything goes wrong (as, of course, it surely will) it may not be seen to be your fault.

Do not let Smug Marrieds get up your nose

They will try. They will try to make you envy them, while in some strange way they would rather not understand, they will know they envy you. But they won't show it. Instead, they'll try to get up your nose.

Do not let them. Confront yourself with the truism that come January, a good deal of these Smug Marrieds will be well down the road to becoming divorced.

Because Christmas can do that, you know. Divorce lawyers never go skiing in January. They rub their hands – and not against the cold. It is the Big Season. Divorce lawyers *always* have a Happy New Year.

But say you are a man.
And you have a mistress.

Hmm...

Or say you are a woman.
And you *are* a mistress.

Hmm...

It's not a good time.

*'You stay right there
while I go and get a divorce...'*

Just how bad depends upon the stage of the relationship, of course. If it's a fairly recent arrangement, then the pain on both sides will be undeniably keen. Because if the rule is (as it is)

You Don't Phone Me At Home,

then the *absolute* rule is

You Don't Phone Me At Home Over Christmas.

Even on the mobile. Except at prearranged moments. During which rushed conversations, one party will say:
'Oh-God-oh-God-oh-God-oh-God I'll *die* if I don't see you *now,* right this moment – what's that noise I can hear? What are you doing?'

And the other party will say,
'Look, it won't be *long,* my darling. It's just a few days. Just count off the minutes like I do.'

And the first party will say,
  'It sounds like laughter to me, that noise.'

And the other party will say,
  'Laughter? No, no. No laughter here. It's
  the dog. Got a cough, or something.'

If, however, the affair is rather longer in the
tooth, then this enforced vacation from one
another is seen to be a blessing on both sides,
no matter how strong the protestations to the
contrary. The two parties simply must
solemnly vow to have no fun whatsoever for
the entire duration and then slope off and
get blasted, in each of their particular ways.

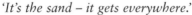

'It's the sand – it gets everywhere.'

Do's and don'ts if you are in a mistress situation

Him

✳ Do give her a very gorgeous present – something she can keep and flaunt.

✳ Do promise her the world, come January. Or February. Anyway, *soon*…

Her

✳ Don't give him any present that cannot be used or consumed immediately (nothing to keep – let alone *flaunt*…).

✳ Do, on your last pre-Christmas encounter, be quite outrageously sexually forthcoming in order to make quite sure that he well knows just what he's missing.

But what with one thing and another, most of us will find ourselves in a family situation, whatever the permutations. Let us address, then…

'I'm betting they prefer the gold
to that other stuff.'

The family

And in particular, the wife and mother (or equivalent). Because right or wrong, it is usually she who deals. Over the years, many men have very cleverly let it be clearly understood that they are perfectly hopeless at actually very simple little matters such as buying things, wrapping things, decorating things, cooking things and taking care of things in general. Other men, of course, are quite simply perfectly hopeless. So it therefore falls to the woman, whether she likes it or not, that one of the first things to be attended to are the…

Christmas cards

Because, do you know: every year she tends to send out more and more (and to whom, exactly? Who are all these bloody people?) and receive fewer and fewer in return. So what's the point? What's the point of sending a card to someone you see all the time? And what's the point of sending a card to someone you haven't seen for decades, and will never see again? As to all those that you can't remember where or how in God's name you even met in the first place... So maybe this year – not bother with cards. Waste of money. Waste of time. And look at the price of the stamps! Then you put away such idle thoughts and go and buy Christmas cards.

Bales of them. Stacks and stacks of those cellophane packs. Charity, if not too gruesome; otherwise, what the hell. And while buying them, you might well spot a perfectly charming...

ADVENT CALENDAR
Buy one if your children clamour and expect it. Do not buy one if every four or five mornings you have to cry out, 'Why has no one been opening the doors on this sodding bloody Advent thing, then? Hey?' (And then you quietly open the doors). And around this time, you will yourself receive in the post the first rush of...

...the early ones always being from those bleeding pests that you actually did this time find the strength of will to knock off your list, God damn them.

And one or two of those cards (you may depend on it) will be harbouring the single most depressing missive it is possible to receive: the round robin end-of-year newsletter from some ceaselessly upbeat and therefore intensely irritating woman whom once you apparently encountered and who seems quite genuinely to imagine that scores of comparative strangers actually give two hoots in blue blazes as to the goings-on of not just her but hers.

Do you *mind* about the emergence of wisdom teeth, the passing (always 'with flying colours') of GCSEs, the lagging of a loft or her wretched husband's sideways promotion? You do not. Obviously, it would be cheering to learn that he'd just been sent down for a fifteen-year stretch, but hard news of that sort never makes it on to these relentlessly self-congratulatory abominations. And do you,

conversely, wish to be apprised of lottery jackpots, a new villa in the Algarve, four holidays a year or a society wedding? Most emphatically not. So the only thing to do with these fab and newsy updates, therefore – and this is particularly true if Kodachrome snaps are in any way involved – is to bin them. Unread. There. You know it makes sense.

But cards *will* keep on arriving, you know, – so now you have to go back to the shops to buy another couple (maybe better make it three) cellophane packs of Christmas cards; but you don't have time to write them now because you really must put in some serious work on that

CHRISTMAS LIST
…which is never easy. And nor are the people involved. Who are always classified as being either

(a) Difficult (b) Impossible

A process of thinning out the no-nos might, at this point, assist you.

Each year, in mid-October, Santa Claus puts on his best uniform and practises his lines in front of a mirror...

Men do **not** want:

1 Turtle Wax (with or without a 'shammy')

2 Toiletry gift sets (particularly those involving any manifestation of deodorant)

3 Bumper packs of razors (particularly if the cellophane pack reads 'Bumper Pack')

4 Homer Simpson bubble bath (or Bart)

5 Sets of spanners (or screwdrivers, or bits)

6 Looney Tunes ties (or socks, or boxers)

7 Shoe-shine kits (particularly in a jokey retro tin)

8 Beer glasses engraved with their names

9 Passport covers (particularly if initialled)

10 Drinking games (even rude ones)

11 Miniature Ferraris (or Porsches, or Mini-Coopers from *The Italian Job*)

12 Key rings of any description whatever

13 A deck of playing cards (or, worse, two)

14 Nose-hair trimmers (enough said)

15 Battery-operated tie-racks (or any other sort)

16 Books of golf jokes (or after-dinner stories)

17 Anything bearing the image of Santa (or the legend 'Ho, Ho, Ho')

18 Electric trouser presses (as ignored in hotels)

19 A 'fun' wine glass that takes a whole bottle

20 Sweatshirts that read 'Under Gardener', 'Galley Slave', 'I Just Work Here', 'Dogsbody', or anything else bloody like it

WOMEN DO **NOT** WANT:

1 Nylon, scratchy underwear (particularly red, or sporting anything like a pom-pom)

2 Any chocolates she sees every day in the supermarket (or worse, 24-hour garage shop)

3 Slimming books or work-out videos (particularly those featuring well-toned women in their forties)

4 Dried-flower arrangements (particularly those in a trug, and flaunting a bow)

5 Tiny cushions smelling of lavender

6 Beatrix Potter figurines (or drawer liners)

7 Treble CDs comprising '100 Ultimate Relaxing Highlights from the Timeless Classics'

8 Steam irons (or the board to go with them)

9 Oven mitts (or kitchen timers – particularly if got up like something they're patently not)

10 Shopping trolleys (or wipe-clean shopping list boards)

11 Candlewick dressing gowns (with or without satin quilted lapels)

12 Ribbon-bound packs of notelets (especially with kittens, fairies or Winnie-the-Pooh)

13 Five-year diaries (even if lockable)

14 Scarf 'n' mitts combos

15 Padded coat hangers (particularly scented)

16 Poinsettias (or hyacinths in clear bowls)

17 Frilly garters

18 Sensible clothing

19 Frivolous clothing

20 A necklace with the slogan 'Mum' (or worse, 'Best Mum in the World')

And what to do if you receive any of these things? In America, what is gaining currency is the...

RE-GIFTING PARTY
...whereby in the first two weeks of January, all unwanted gifts are carefully rewrapped and given to someone else. In Britain, of course, this has been happening forever; we merely wait until the following December.

Later in this section, there is more positive information on the present front. But for now, other things loom. In the last post, in addition to a couple more Christmas cards – one very thick and funereal from your solicitor, the other (featuring a kangaroo in sunglasses) from someone called Stanley in Canberra – you have received the very first flush of...

INVITATIONS
One is from your partner's firm – and you know that your partner will expect you to attend the event if not with joy alive in your heart, then at least in the spirit of grinning

and bearing it. One more invitation is from the People-Next-Door-But-One – which is silly, quite frankly, because you were only just *talking* to them the other morning, so why didn't they tell you then? (Have to have them back, I suppose...). And the third is from School. Inviting you to the Nativity Play and the Carol Service. Which brings into ultra-sharp focus...

'Thanks. We can give it to your father tomorrow.'

CHILDREN

Your children. Not, of course, that they are ever very far from your thoughts. But at this time of year, it all becomes really quite intense.

Because it is, isn't it? A time for children? Ask anyone, and that's what they will tell you. 'Christmas is a time for children,' they'll say (particularly if they don't have to *do* it). Right, then: let's concentrate for now on the children.

In theory, they are very easy to buy for and cater to, because for them it is the build-up that is largely the thing. It's generally a case of

*'Shall I text it, e-mail it,
or stick it up the chimney?'*

coaxing them down gently from premature and unwarrantable heights of excitement and piloting them firmly on the straight and narrow – steering a steady course, in short, between maintaining their levels of gleeful anticipation and seeing to it that they do not spontaneously combust. As to what they *want*... well, everything on the entire planet Earth (and that's just for starters).

But what they *mainly* want, of course, you will already know about. You will already know about it because they will have been telling and telling and telling you every single day (and not just the once) in increasingly clamorous tones – and when the thing is yet once more screamingly promoted during the endless and lucrative punctuations in their favourite TV programmes, the fevered yearning soars into overdrive, the need for this thing propelling the child to teeter upon the brink of explosion.

And what *is* this thing? I'll tell you.

It is...

THE TOY OF THE YEAR

Because there is one every year. The must-have. The make or break. The winner. And every year this is how it goes:

(a) In October, it is in short supply. And as early as October, of course, you have yet to hear anything about it.

(b) In November, it is pretty much nowhere to be had.

(c) In December, a rumour that just four were spotted in a Toys-'R'-Us one hundred and fifty miles from your home town is to prove unfounded. You know this, because, along with scores of others, you made the drive (the hapless manager only narrowly avoiding a lynching).

And I would add:

(d) In January, it is all over the bloody place – knee-deep and yours for the taking.

This is not only both maddening and depressing, but also not the point because the child wants it and wants it NOW. And so, curiously, do you – it has become a mission.

Wide-eyed and with a rather frightening determination, you stalk the malls and the more out-of-town precincts and the department stores and even the markets. And should you spot the Holy Grail and a rival tigress already has her paws about it, you will, without so much as a qualm, rip out her throat and proffer your Visa. That is, of course, *if* you spot one.

Anyway, good luck in your quest.

But meanwhile, on the next page is a list of stuff to avoid – more of a help to uncles and aunties and nans and granddads and other assorted fringe outsiders who are Not In The Know. Parents themselves are both brainwashed and indoctrinated. You can tell by their glassy and elsewhere stares.

TEN THINGS CHILDREN DO **NOT** WANT

1 Board games (unless pertaining to the latest film or TV fantastical idiocy)

2 Jigsaws (obviously)

3 Games of skill (or, indeed, anything else in this genre, unless it plugs in or requires around a dozen AA batteries and generally makes one hell of a bloody noise)

4 Unpainted, beautifully crafted wooden traditional toys (particularly if they don't even have wheels)

5 Clothes. Unless

  (**a**) for girls: Sparkly

  (**b**) for boys: Black

6 One of those miniature wheelbarrows, or a trowel and watering can set (or anything else that even so much as hints at work of any kind whatever)

7 Premium Bonds (be real)

8 The Complete Works of Shakespeare (oh pleeease!)

9 Walkie-talkies (Duhhh! Like they don't already have those nifty state-of-the-art, colour-screen, text-sending mobiles with built-in digital cameras?)

10 Chocolates or biscuits. These are a Given. They will be Around. They do not constitute A Present.

The most common errors of all, of course, are to buy them something

(a) far too young ('What do you think I am? A, like – *baby*?')

(b) far too advanced ('What do you mean you're going to put it away until I'm older? I want to wreck it *now*!')

(c) just *so* last year ('Oh, my God – are they still *making* these things? I don't even know where all mine are, now')

There follows a list of what they *do* want. But be warned: the days of saving up and waiting are long gone. If they ever wanted it, they've probably got it by now.

That said:

GIRLS

✳ Barbie (sorry – they just love her. New issues only, though).

✳ Kits for making horrid things such as candy floss, liquid chocolate, popcorn or cookies. (Caution: they expect you to not just eat the result, but also go 'Yum, yum'.)

✳ Soft toys. Whatever they say, they can't resist. At any age. (Quality, though – and the bigger the better.)

✳ The most fashionable hair or body accessory of the season (tread very carefully here).

✳ Sylvanian Families (if you don't know, find out).

✳ A shopping trip with Mum plus best friend to choose the clothes they really, really want.

✳ A proper little armchair she can sit in. And later, nestle together all her favourite dolls and softies. And later still, keep forever.

✳ A pretty locket or bracelet – not trashy, but neither so valuable that she's Not Allowed To Wear It.

✳ A dressing table with a lit-up mirror, ruched curtains beneath and lots of secret drawers, one of them containing a lockable jewel box.

✳ A pony. Or else, to be a ballerina (yes, still).

BOYS

✳ Scalextric. Women just don't understand this – and curse when they trip all over the damn thing. Men, however, understand all too well. And they pine when eventually it is consigned to the attic.

✳ Connecting sets involving strong and brightly coloured magnets.

✳ Lego sets that don't look like toys so much as serious equipment.

✳ Action Man (though they may not care to admit it. Particularly if you ever catch sight of the thing in the sister's Barbie pink convertible).

✳ Bicycles. But God help you if you don't
  (a) research,
  (b) consult,
  (c) get all the extras.

✳ An airgun. (Yes, I *know* you haven't the slightest intention of getting him any such thing and that they should be banned – but such a thing is, believe me, what he wants.)

* The latest and most desirable computer game. This will involve noise and violence, of course. Note, however, the words 'latest' and 'most desirable' (this means, basically, that all his friends want, but so far none has got: be quick).

* The very newest strip with all accessories, including football, *pertaining to the club of his choice*.

* A darts set. Or an archery set. Or an assagai set. Any pin-sharp propellant, basically, that is potentially lethal.

* A proper electric-powered Aston Martin that they actually sit in and which can top 25 mph and everything about it works. Or else, to be James Bond (yes, still).

Following that bout of virtual shopping, you might now care to pause for a breather. Trouble is, this will give you time to think – and then you might just find yourself casting a nervous glance in the direction of your budget. For you will have gamely drawn one up (and vowed to stick to it), but just now you are experiencing some qualms because already (and Jesus: you've barely got going) it is becoming more and more horribly apparent that this budget of yours is really little more than a rather bad joke.

Oh, dear.

Let us see the thing through by addressing the highly contentious issue of the...

CHRISTMAS STOCKING
Not just because the gathering of all the bits and pieces necessary is another damn job in itself (and it is); nor because all these so-called cheap little stocking fillers have a way of adding up to an absolute bomb (and they do); but because to go through with the thing again this year will be either to

perpetuate a treasured tradition (and tell me: do you still get out the same old handed-down, frayed and much-loved stocking? Or maybe the little smashers have now traded up to duvet covers?) or else face up to the passing of the years and have done with the whole charade.

In short, what do you so when they say to you: 'Mummy... (or 'Daddy...)

...IS SANTA CLAUS REAL?'

Your instinct is to rush to assure them that of course he's real – whatever put it into your head that he might not be? And there we have the rub: something or someone *did* put it into their heads, clearly, so what are you going to do about it? Here are some alternatives:

(a) Act shifty
(b) Feed the doubt
(c) Confirm the awful truth
(d) Be thoroughly grown-up about it and lie through your teeth

The more liberal among you will be cheered to hear that there exists another way: *prove it*.

Yes. Don't just *say* that Santa exists; *prove* it. Banish all trace of their doubts (which is all they really want you to do). Get them to compose their lists to Santa well in advance (having, very prudently, urged upon them considerable restraint) and then set about fulfilling them. Because you knew pretty much *anyway*, didn't you? (The Toy of the Year, for a start). That way, everyone (and all beliefs) emerge intact. And don't forget to get down you the mince pie and cherry brandy that will be thoughtfully (and with great reverence) laid out for the Great Man on that night of nights, Christmas Eve. Because it's only polite.

But even if you decide to prove it, there arise complications from other quarters – notably, your chum and mine, the department store. If an excursion to the Grotto is on the agenda, will they truly believe that the white-bearded school-leaver, aglow with sweat and nerves within his very voluminous crimson robes is, in fact, the real deal?

It's a tricky one. And particularly so if they've just spotted *another* Santa in the street outside. Lurking, too, is the danger that, when in-store Santa asks the little mites what they want for Christmas (and just how irresponsible is *that*?) they might take it into their little heads to change their minds and reel off a new list altogether. The hazard is best avoided by simply letting them espy some dear old Santa from afar (cheaper, too; and you don't have to queue).

So, with one more burden dealt with (leaving the women now with just a few more hundred to go) it is time to turn our attention to

THE MAN'S SHARE

Which, as we have seen, he will have been earnestly whittling down to as slender as possible – sometimes to the point of whip-thin invisibility. He doesn't mind buying a Christmas tree (strapping it onto the roof rack, as he might a freshly felled elk) and he might even stretch to making the thing as firm as a rock in bin or bucket (man's work, you see – women simply wouldn't grasp the principle, here), but he is damned if he is going to drape upon it anything akin to tinsel or baubles: nothing of that nature – God, no.

He will also baulk at a visit to the shops to buy anything at all for his children, parents, secretary or friends (or, come to that, a visit to the shops for any single purpose whatever; this can be meanness, but far more often it is merely sheer indolence, deftly woven into and around a gross misapplication of machismo). What he simply *cannot* get out of, however, is buying a present for his significant other.

Which is easier than he might imagine. We have already seen what it is he must avoid. It is wise also to thoroughly rule out

(a) the hastily scribbled out cheque,

(b) the Interflora cop-out,

(c) the desperately, seized-upon coffret of 5pm-on-Christmas-Eve Chanel No 5 *eau de toilette* and bath foam.

The following is more the direction he should be looking.

Lingerie

Important caveat: know your woman. If she does not regularly disport herself about the house in diaphanous purple teddies or magenta satin crotchless knickers, there is a reason: she does not work in a cathouse.

So – stick to black, white or champagne, make sure it is of the highest quality, sexy but wearable, and the right size. Pointing at a sales assistant's bosom and muttering that 'She's, um – your sort of shape, only smaller...} simply won't do. Think in terms of Janet Reger, Agent Provocateur or Rigby & Peller.

Important tip: if you hold your nerve until around the 20th December (not too difficult, for the average man), the better sorts of lingerie shops will slash their prices, pour you a glass of Champagne, and wrap up all the frillies quite beautifully. Worth knowing.

Her favourite scent

Not the one you have unthinkingly bought for years and years, and now the cupboard is jammed with it. No – go for the type she *really* loves (it's the one she uses seldom, because there's so little left). And make it *scent* – not the watered-down variety, nor all the over-boxed offshoots of nothing at all.

*'How **COULD** you give me a food mixer for Christmas?!'*

A generous gift token to…

…somewhere splendid, where (after Christmas) she can indulge herself in an orgy of massage, plunge baths, saunas, facials, makeovers, pedicures, exfoliation – all the things that (after Christmas) she'll be convinced she badly needs.

Cashmere

This is tried and tested. Simple styling, please; avoid both patterns and primary colours. Important tip: sales of the better stuff often start up in late December.

Chocolates

Not the ones she sees daily in the supermarket and garage shop – no. Exclusive, superbly boxed and lavish, please: Prestat, Charbonnel et Walker and Ackerman's will all go down very well.

IMPORTANT WARNING: do not buy chocolates *of any description whatever* if she is currently struggling to convince herself that she is in the middle of a diet.

A handbag

Wait wait *wait* – not just *any* handbag. Are you mad? This needs work. There are some women who physically *ache* for the bag of the moment – which, in common with The Toy of the Year, is usually virtually unobtainable. Secure it, and you'll become in her eyes no less than a demigod. It'll cost you, though. The actual makes change with the season; Prada and Hermès are usually safe, though.

Important warning: another sort of woman will scorn such nonsense – and if she discovered what you had *paid* for the thing would condemn you for a fool. And then she'll take it back: an action which both parties, generally, are anxious to avoid.

Jewellery

…if she's a jewellery kinda gal. Wives tend not to want diamonds (yahoo!); they'd far rather the money went on relagging the loft, or reducing the mortgage. But something elegant and fine *in the right box* (high-street jewellers are a no-no) might just ring her bell. Cartier is still the favourite, but Bulgari and Tiffany are by no means to be sneered at. Upmarket costume jewellery from Dior and Chanel is currently in favour – and Butler & Wilson is always a good (and more economical) bet.

A cornucopia of good little things

A well-framed photo of the children (one you took in secret); candles imbued in her favourite scent; a dozen pairs of tights by such as Fogal, in a colour she wears; kid gloves so fine you could pull them through a curtain ring. And all this hand-wrapped by you – which I know could cost you a weekend's fumbling and swearing, but she'll appreciate the result, no matter how inept: trust me.

You might further, by way of a pre-Christmas bonus, consider taking the lady somewhere rather good for lunch or dinner… but you must think through the consequences.

Firstly, she might turn you down flat.

Women can do this.

She will have been vociferously protesting against her 24-hour non-stop diet of responsibility and chores, but will still laugh in the face of this offer of respite.

'How on *earth* do you think I can make the time to dawdle over *food* in some stupid and overpriced restaurant?! I have a 24-hour non-stop diet of responsibility and *chores*!'

Or, conversely (with women, there is always a converse 'or' to be considered), she might leap at the chance.
But.
If lunch is the order of the day, there are two things to be wary of:

1 No matter how smart the venue, during December there will be several tables pushed together to accommodate some or other office do. These are seriously bad news. Balloons might well be present. Crackers most certainly will be. As could those gismos with a feather on the end that you blow through and they sound like musical, if off-key, farts.

And the 'do' will outlast your lunch, so there's no release. You will have to speak too loudly in order to compensate for all the red-face and phoney festive *bonhomie* and lechery; the waiters will devote to the party their total attention (because the party is spending much more than you are – just look at all those bottles!). All of this is initially merely irritating, but ultimately very lowering indeed.

2 The woman might brightly suggest having just the one course and skipping coffee and let's get out of here, why don't we, because...

'There's this dress I really want you to see.'

Caught.

Can't claim a prior engagement, can you? You are trussed and stuffed, mate. You will soon find yourself on a chair, in a shop, awaiting her egress from the changing room. And every time she emerges she will be twirling about in a different creation.

You, however, must each and every time say The Same Thing. Which is:

'Very nice.'

That's it. Don't go *into* it. Don't, for God's sake, *elaborate*. And never point out a drawback; if there is one, she already knows. If asked about how any single part of her anatomy is looking, what you say is:

'Very nice.'

Because no part of her (with the exception of breasts) must ever be said to look *big*. And remember – she's only showing you the dresses for form's sake. She has already decided which she is buying. You will, of course, be expected to pay – which may not be very nice at all – but hey! What are you going to do? If it is just the one dress (and no frightening mentions of things like Manolos and Choos) you have got off rather lightly.

Because, of course, come Christmas, she already knows exactly what she will be wearing for each and every event: the drinks with the People-Next-Door-But-One, the firm's Christmas party, the Nativity Play, Christmas Day, Boxing Day, New Year's Eve – the lot. She might even feel provoked into asking you what *you* will be wearing on all these days. If so, you simply supply the truth. You say that you *haven't really given it a great deal of thought,* save for the fact that if she gives you a couple of ties, you'll put on one of those. The truth that she will

demand to know what exactly is wrong with the *other* one does not, at this juncture, really bear thinking about. Both of the ties, you say, are

'Very nice'

...and leave it at that.

And despite the fact that she is daily declaiming that her allocated budget for the festive season may be seen to be a little more than the most pitiful joke, what you would like her to buy for *you* is as follows.

1 Complete DVDs of your secret pleasure – which might well be anything from *Buffy the Vampire Slayer* (your delight in this series serving to disgust your children because you are so chronically and horribly *old*) to endless replays of the greatest sporting achievements that the world has seen *ever*.

2 A really discreet but superb 'writing instrument' as they call them, these days. Not a fountain pen (which you'll never use) but a ballpoint (which you will).

3 A year's subscription to *Playboy*. Not just because it now comes with a stamp of approval (as well as every month), but because of the endless delight you will experience when telling your friends that, for Christmas, your partner got you a year's subscription to *Playboy*! (Must be *Playboy*, though – anything that is thought to be similar simply isn't: too tacky for words.)

4 Fine wine. Really good stuff – and French, obviously. Or fine malt whisky or Cognac – or fine anything else that you like to get down you. And maybe some Havanas.

5 A token for an 'experience'. But pray to God that she reads you right. A parachute jump is of no use to the vertiginous, and nor are twenty laps in a Formula One McLaren if you've recently lost your licence (this due, maybe, to the fine wine, malt whisky, Cognac or fine anything else that you like to get down you).

6 Shirts. Not ties – shirts. The best ones: Hilditch & Key. And blue. So you'll wear them.

7 Books and records. But there's no room for slip-ups, here. Make a list in good time and give it to her. Not too exciting or romantic, but look: you get the books and records you want.

8 A beautiful, but *beautiful*, soft and lacy bra and panties and suspender belt and seamed stockings and high heels combo. (On *her* – not *you*, dummy).

And that for now, is the man's share dealt with. Got off lightly, the men, didn't they really? Either way, it's back to the...

'Well, at least the conception
was immaculate...'

WOMAN OF THE HOUSE

And time is passing, and don't you think she isn't very aware of the fact. December is nearly half done and so, by God, is she.

But there is still so much to attend to. Every time she thinks she has achieved something (ticked something off the endless list), instead of a glow within, all she can feel are by no means the very first stirrings of unease; such feelings, now, are her permanent bedfellows. They stalk her in the night. And I'll tell you what's preying on her mind:

1 Is it too stupidly early to order the turkey? Because I've read about this very special breed called something like 'bronze' (which doesn't, does it, sound as if it's going to be very tender?) that you can have throttled and gutted to order from some little farm in the Orkneys, or somewhere. But quite frankly, when it comes down to it, I'll probably order from the supermarket, as per usual. The trouble is, this early and they say it's too early. But soon all the best ones are booked – and then, oh God, it's too late. So maybe order it now (safe side) and then confirm the order *every single subsequent morning.*

2 And talking of food – what about all the *rest* of the cooking? Hey? One seems to be cooking all the bloody *time*, no matter how much cold stuff and nuts and so on one keeps on laying in. And what if the turkey is (oh, God, I can't stand it) – *dry*? I'd rather die. Look, all I want here is *perfection* in everything. That's all I need. The presents, the decorations, the children's delight, the peace, the love, the sheer bleeding goodwill – and of *course* the sodding turkey. Perfection is all I want. God in heaven: is that too much to *ask*?!

3 What if I can't get slots at the hairdresser? You try to book early and they say it's too early. I'll need to go not

just on Christmas Eve, but on the day of the firm's party and the day of drinks with the People-Next-Door-But-One and the day of the Nativity Play – and then again in good time for New Year and – oh God Almighty: supposing I just can't get the slots? I think I'll book them all now anyway (safe side) and then confirm the bookings *every single subsequent morning*.

4 And mention of the Nativity Play has reminded me again: I'm supposed to be making a *costume*. I know that some mothers just hire them from one of those theatrical places, but the cost for just – what? Half-an-hour on stage? Ridiculous. Plus, it may be OK if your child has been cast as Joseph or Mary or Herod or just some loon-faced shepherd – even the bloody *manger*. But this Christmas – nothing like that. Not even a sheep or an ox. Do you know what my child is down to be this year? A blade of grass. No, I am *not* joking! A blade of grass. So how do I go about that,

in a sane world? It's very silly, anyway, because he's tall for his age, my one, and what sort of blade of grass is it, please tell me, that towers over all three kings put together? (Each of them, incidentally, played by perfectly horrid little boys, actually, but their parents I happen to know for a fact are of course very well in with the *teacher...*)

And to all such worries, I say this: *relax*. Ah, you protest. Easy for you to say. But listen: relax, because in your heart of hearts you just know it will all work out in the end, don't you? Because

(a) You've put so much damn work into it.

(b) It always does. Somehow or other.

But. A word of warning about newspapers at this time of year. All the columnists for some reason will have been urged to write on seasonal matters; they seek to stuff us to the gills. Now, these columns, apart from being money for old rope (they're all the same as last year and the year before), they can serve to wrongfoot you. Try to filter out and read (if you really have to) only those that tell you how utterly crap the writer's Christmas is destined to be. With lurid evidence. Or those that recall in lovingly sadistic detail all the calamities of yesteryear.

Avoid, on the other hand, all those articles by overpaid harpies with lucrative contracts and merchant-banker husbands and a fleet of nannies who wonder aloud and at length why it is that the so-called 'womanhood' of this so-called country of ours at this oh-so-special time of year does nothing but bitch and *whinge*.

And avoid in particular any columnists sufficiently cruel as to tell you that they are going away this year, because this you really do not wish to know.

Do not either, by the way, worry that you have not bought enough. You have. You have bought enough of everything to enable you to not just withstand a siege, but to fortify a coming crusade. What you do now have to turn your attention to, however, is the…

CHRISTMAS TREE

And the first thing you should bear in mind is that this merry little task will take you at least twice as long as your most generous estimate. Even if you're dragging out the same old artificial Noble Fir from its dusty cubby hole and placing on it the same old lights and the same old baubles in the same old places, the job will write off the thicker end of the afternoon, and could well take you into the evening.

And when you are feeling none too happy at the top of a pair of steps and straining your arm to steady up the same old tatty fairy, it is entirely possible that the doorbell will ring and you will call out,

'Answer That, Someone, Will You?'

And the doorbell will ring again, and you might well shriek out,

'Have You All Gone *Deaf*?

There's Someone At The Bloody *Door*!'

And then, when it rings again, you shall swear and cuss and come down from the ladder and stamp into the hall and wrench open the door and be confronted by a neat little apple-cheeked gaggle of

CAROL SINGERS
And they will start up on *Good King Wenceslas* and the freezing air is rushing into the hall but you don't like to slam the door in their faces, poor little lambs, so you simper a bit and you half-close the door and you rush upstairs and scramble around for your purse and then call out,

'Has Anyone Got A Pound? *Hel-lo*? A **Pound**? *Anyone*? God Almighty, Has Everyone *Died* or Something?'

(And all this shouting can be very enervating; even more of a worry, all this, if you live on your own, of course). And then you come down with a tenner and you press it into the hand of the eldest-looking caroller and you are not sure which of you is the more amazed by this thing you have just done because going through the heads of the two of you is this:

*Bloody hell! A **tenner**!*

In exchange for which, it is soon made clear, you are eligible for subjection to their entire melodic repertoire – but not if you can help it, *matey*, because you've got the door shut tight now and you're standing there feeling spare and thinking:

Now what on earth was it I was doing?

And then you think:

Oh, yeah – bloody fairy.

YOU ARE ADVISED to buy a real tree, by the way, for the following reasons:

1 They smell nice. Like Badedas.

2 You are forced to rethink the dispersal of baubles – it's very far from symmetrical.

3 It dissuades the children from urging you to buy a pure-white, holographic, fibre-optic and quite laughably expensive job they saw in the department store. Next year, believe me, they will take one look at it and go, 'Oh yuk – gross'.

4 When the time comes to dismantle the thing, there is (despite cascades of needles even from trees guaranteed to produce no such thing) a grim satisfaction to be had from getting the thing out of the house and done with (for another year).

Once it is dressed and the family assembled, their mouths ready-pouted for the collective 'Ooooooh...!' following the ritual turning on of the lights (and despite the cliché to the contrary, they almost always do work), you will be hoping that you experience: The *buzz*. The *kick*. The very first stirrings of *excitement*. That thing they call the...

CHRISTMAS SPIRIT
...which, as you grow older, comes upon you later and later. Sometimes not till bedtime on Christmas Eve. Sometimes you can still be waiting in hopeless anticipation come Shrove Tuesday. But if it's going to come early, then Christmas Tree-time is as good a bet as any.

And talking of Christmas Eve, it will, believe me, be along in no time. You go from having simply sprawling ages of time to none at all in the merest twinkling. But long before then you have *functions* to attend. The first of which being the Firm's Christmas Party

Or, worse: the Office Party

Or, worse still: BOTH.

TIPS FOR **MEN** ATTENDING THE FIRM'S CHRISTMAS PARTY

1 Do not, beforehand, even begin to suggest to your partner what might be suitable attire for the occasion. She will have, as we have seen, already and very laboriously decided on that, down to the smallest accessory.

2 When she appears and is ready to leave and maybe even does a little twirl, what you say is: 'Very Nice'. Or even: 'Beautiful'.

3 Do not drive. You know that the firm's Christmas party is not at all the place to get wasted, but you know, too, that you will need a good few bracers just to get through it (and especially if that swine from Marketing is up to all his old tricks: you know the one I mean).

4 Order a cab beforehand to get you home by eleven at the latest. Because come ten-thirty, you will either be desperate to make your exit or else quite keen to linger. Alcohol-fuelled and festive lust might just be stalking you; you are sure that newish young secretary has been eyeing you for ages. She very probably hasn't – but if she has, then be assured: so has your partner. Get in the cab. No ifs or buts: just get in the cab.

5 Try to appear responsible, but not as a stuffed shirt. Try to be a little bit merry, but far from abandoned. You will fail in all of this, but try.

6 Do not insist that your partner cleave to you at all times, but neither must you leave her stranded. And especially not if that swine from Marketing is up to all his old tricks. You know the one I mean.

TIPS FOR **WOMEN** ATTENDING THE FIRM'S CHRISTMAS PARTY

1 Try not to dress up to the point were other women gleefully whisper *Where Does She Think She Is? Buckingham Palace?* Nor so trashily that the swine from Marketing makes a beeline for you with a couple of rum punches and addresses your chest.

2 Do not say to your partner, while awaiting the cab to get there (because neither of you is driving) anything along the lines of:

(a) 'There is a *pressed* suit in the wardrobe, you know'

(b) 'Are you seriously thinking of wearing *that* tie?'

3 Be gracious to the boss-figure. Not gushing – gracious. Do not ignore the women, but neither must you say to any of them:

(a) 'God, what have you done to yourself?'

(b) 'Have you lost weight?'

(c) 'Oh you look marvellous! I've always loved that dress!'

4 Do not keep a firm hold of your partner's elbow at all times. It is permissible to make your presence felt, however, when

(a) the swine from Marketing becomes really quite intolerable

(b) the newish young secretary (who's been eyeing your man for ages) makes her move.

5 Try to appear loyal and dutiful, and not as if you're there because you have to be. Try to be feminine and flattering but not too flirtatious. You will fail in all of this, but try.

6 When the cab arrives, leave. Do not listen if your partner says to you that the night is young and you can always get another cab later: leave.

OFFICE PARTIES

...are subtly different. Here – where you are all employees mucking in together, so to speak, there is more room for leeway. Do not get so smashed, however, that you do anything at all that others can exact huge delight from retailing to yet more people avid to hear it (on and on and way into January). If you witness such behaviour in others, of course, be merciless.

Good King Wenceslas
looked out of it

Concerning the mistletoe nightmare

Office parties are about the only place you'll come across the dreaded parasite, these days. Should you find yourself trapped beneath it in a potentially smoochy situation with someone very horribly old and/or ugly and/or drunk, take the following evasive action.

Tell them that mistletoe is highly poisonous (true). Then pluck a berry from the branch and challenge them to prove you wrong. They will either scarper or laugh at you. Either way, the moment has passed.

Totally different, quite naturally, are the...

DRINKS WITH THE PEOPLE-NEXT-DOOR-BUT-ONE

You have to, at the outset, understand why you are here. Not for the *drinks*, obviously (you've got your own drinks next door but one: where already you yearn to return). You are here:

1 To admire whatever home improvements have recently been put in hand, in addition to any new acquisitions. (And you *will* admire them, even if you're thinking *My God – What Sort of Person Would Lay Out Good Money On **THAT**?*).

2 To become in their debt, so that come New Year (or at the latest, Easter), you will feel constrained to have them troop into your house in order to witness all your endeavours on similar fronts. Or, more likely, the absence of same. Either way, you're caught.

Console yourself. When such grisly occasions arise, at least you don't have to worry about transport home. As to conversation: very much on parochial lines, of course.

School

Bring this up if you're going private. Say that of course it costs an absolute bomb, but if you can't invest in your own children's futures, then what sort of a parent does that make you?

Resist the compulsion, however, strong, to tell them of your children's various brilliances and successes, even if

(**a**) they are genuine

(**b**) you qualify your remarks by simpering Not That It's Really For Me To Say So...

Property

The price rises/falls, which are quite amazing/ wicked, depending upon the hugeness or otherwise of your mortgage, the looming of negative equity and/or the smug knowledge of your other little place, in the Cotswolds.

The bin men

Who always call to wish you a Happy Christmas and stick out their horrible hands. It's the only time of year when they don't hurl the bins back from the length of the street. You may marvel upon how they must pine for the days of heavy and galvanized bins, when the potential for serious noise and damage must have been considerable.

After a decent interval (more than ten minutes, less than two hours) make your excuses and leave. Blame your having to drag yourself away on the children or the sitter or the cat or – if you have to – the merest touch of dyspepsia; just say it's been playing up for days: nerves, you expect.

And talking of nerves – there are no nerves like those you experience while attending the...

Nativity play

...and not least because they won't let you book seats. No matter now early you snip off that little reply coupon thing and send it off with your cheque (I know! They say is goes to charity...), you still have to take pot luck on the door. Which generally means an appalling scrum around forty-five minutes before kick-off (no fun at all in an icy gale – because have you ever known a school open a bloody door before the appointed hour?

And even when you are seated actually quite near the front – with, of course, the usual giant bang in front of you, or else that woman who habitually comes to anything in one of those stupid hats – your nerves are due to be strummed again when the teacher comes on and announces a slight delay. And no matter that all the parents chuckle good-humouredly, in the hearts and minds of each of them is this worry: is my child ill? Has he fallen down the trap door? Has he got stage-fright? Not a nose-bleed again, please God...

But it's OK now. It's all right. The piano has started up and the curtains are juddering apart and so now you can put away all the worry and settle back again into good old nerves because, you know – you want your child to do *well*, don't you? So. There is Mary, look (sweet little girl) and there is Joseph (always gets the good parts, that boy; don't know who he is, but I've got a good idea) and there are the Three Wise Men (one of them in what looks very like this season's Versace)... and then you go:

AAAAAH!

Because *look* – at the back. See him? Behind all the sheep. See him? To the left of that could-be bullock. Yes, it's him – see him now? Your very own Christmas blade of grass.

'Yes, Mary, you look lovely, but DO try and remember not to hold Jesus like that.'

Isn't he adorable? And so *what*, actually, if all you could eventually think of when push came to shove was to truss him up in a couple of bog-green bin bags? What else were you expected to do? And you wish that that very annoying man would sit down. The man with the teeny camcorder who keeps on bobbing and crouching and generally behaving as if he's Cecil B. De Mille, or something. And actually – there are loads of them, now you come to look: all these fathers in straight-from-the-office, boring suits and faintly stubbly jawlines, their rictus smiles set behind their cameras.

And at first you think:
*Oh God how **VULGAR**, how show-offy – how typical of this school.*

And then you think:
I wonder if I could get hold of a copy from one of them?

Cecil B. De Mille, conceivably.

Because it would be nice, wouldn't it? To keep. For when your little man is a Daddy himself, with blades of grass of his own. And afterwards, you know – he is so excited by the boards and greasepaint that it is all you can do to get the bin bags off him: he says he wants to wear them for ever and ever and certainly on Christmas Eve for when

SANTA COMES

Ah, yes indeed. The big one – the day when it all begins to make some sense: Christmas Eve. Not, however, if you are one of those people who attend to everything stupidly late. For this is the day when they finally stir themselves. Not the women, usually. They might rack their brains for anything they might have forgotten, sure (Baco-Foil? Got it. Bread? Got enough bread to build a wholemeal wall…).

But some *men* – oh dear oh dear oh dear. This day, it surely seems, enough Chanel No 5 is sold to flood the Thames Basin. It has the benefit, you see, of being not just memorable and famously expensive and also

'Times are tough, so stop
moaning and get used to it.'

ready-wrapped, but also (unlike a good many) pronounceable.

As we have seen, however, such last minute and thoughtless behaviour is very much frowned upon. Don't do it. Because if you do, you just know that you're going to hate yourself in the morning when she, as usual, sniffs at the package, and lays it aside. But there is much, much more to...

CHRISTMAS EVE

...than frantic and guilt-ridden present-buying. There are, of course, the Traditions. Maybe just the one. A certain supper – Welsh Rarebit, say – or the final indulgent takeaway before the onslaught of serious cookery. Perhaps a favourite seasonal film or two. *Scrooge* is a good one. But the best by a mile is *It's a Wonderful Life*, because you will cry with joy at the end. This film will put you in the mood, and go a long way to ensuring that you get *the buzz*, and that you go to bed feeling relatively buoyant, and not weighed down by a lowering awareness of all you must face in the morning.

For some, Midnight Mass is the ultimate tradition. It's a good one if

(a) Your place of worship is walkable
(b) You can stay awake long enough to see it through
(c) It is not merely an excuse to rush home afterwards and open all your presents in the middle of the night.

The tradition to end them all, though, has to involve your little blade of grass. It is, of course, the hanging up of the

CHRISTMAS STOCKING

Sometimes, it's not a stocking at all (the manufacturers of pillowslips have a great deal to answer for). And often it's not hung, either (nails in the mantelpiece or bedhead? I don't really think so). But however you do it, the thrill and the expectation are the same. Because, listen...

Santa is coming with...

(and you *have* attended to it, haven't you?)

...lots of toys and goodies for all the good girls and boys.

CHRISTMAS EVE POINTERS

1 It is advisable to wrap up each little stocking knick-knack individually – a very satisfying way, incidentally, of using up all those scraps of Christmas paper that were just that bit too big to throw away. Not only will this fuel the children's anticipation, but it will also make the whole business of ripping into it last a bit longer. And as most parents would agree, the more protracted the distraction the better.

2 It is not really advisable, however, for the Man of the House to go the whole hog and actually dress up as Father Christmas and bang around the place in the middle of the night for the following reasons:

(a) The beard will tickle you damnably

(b) You will wake them up. And not only are they not meant to lay eyes on Santa, but they will have no hope whatever of ever getting back to sleep

(c) They might recognize you – and they surely will if you walk into a door and swear, the way you do

3 As to the mince pies and cherry brandy, or whatever *bonne bouche* has been lovingly and reverentially laid out for Santa: make sure they are no longer there in the morning. You don't have to consume them; just get them out of the way (although leaving the dregs in the glass and a few crumbs on the plate demonstrates a tender touch, and can instil wonder).

Right, then. I think that's about all you can do, just for now. Do we agree that you've earned a good night's rest? I thought so. Turn off the lights (leaving the Christmas tree till last – a secret delight) and get the door locked up for the night. Now you can join the angels in a sweet and scented slumber.

God knows you'll need it.

Because tomorrow (as if I have to tell you) it is finally come:

Christmas!

2

simply having a
wonderful christmastime

So – it's Christmas morning. Exactly what *time* on Christmas morning, of course, depends very largely upon your domestic situation. If children are involved, then beyond the windows it is as black as night; could still *be* night, of course – but more likely it is around pre-dawn.

What you must *not* do:
1 Say to your little darlings 'Go back to sleep.'

2 Attempt to go back to sleep yourself. You wouldn't, anyway, because your mind is now teeming with things (not least getting started in on the turkey).

3 Attempt to rouse your partner. Because he just won't budge. It's hopeless.

Now, at this point there are many ways of proceeding; ritual and tradition will always play a part. But here's a suggestion:

The Woman of the House greets the yelps of excitement from the children with a good deal of enthusiasm (even if she feels sledge-hammered: this is Christmas Day, after all). And while she attends to perfectly disgusting things at this ungodly time of day (giblets, you know, are hardly famous for taking care of themselves), the children can start in on their stockings (once the fire is going and the tree's alight).

Meanwhile…

The Man of the House is sleeping.
Or pretending to.

WARNING: it is important to make the contents of the stocking last, as has already been said. As each little thing is unwrapped, therefore, insist that it is examined, tried out and thoroughly appreciated. Preferably twice.

Meanwhile…

The Man of the House is sleeping.
Or pretending to.

Once the dead weight of the bird has been just about jammed into the oven, a lightish breakfast has to be seen to. Orange juice. Croissants. Maybe scrambled eggs. Coffee. At the first whiff of which the Man of the House is sleeping no longer.

No pretence about it.

He comes down, now – jollies around with the kiddies, happy to assume both credit and command.

This is the time for you to join them. You might wish to dress at this point. Bit of hair and make-up, maybe (this is Christmas Day, after all).

'Hi you guys! What are we having for Christmas din...'

NOTES FOR THE MAN OF THE HOUSE

1 Open a bottle of Champagne. It doesn't matter that it's early; look at the woman: she needs a sharpener. Run your tongue across your unspeakably furry palate: so do you. Open a bottle of Champagne.

2 Do not ignore the children's silly little toys from Santa.

3 More important: do not commandeer them, either.

4 You might wish to dress at this point. Bit of a shave and hair-comb, maybe (this is Christmas Day, after all).

NOTES FOR THE WOMAN
OF THE HOUSE

1 Are any relatives due over? Parents, aged aunts, that sort of thing? If so, enjoy to the full these precious Champagne and stocking-filler moments while they remain. The rest of the day will be fine, but different.

2 Do, please, cast from your mind all your determination to achieve on this day of days 'perfection' by bearing in mind that:

(a) All idyllic (usually American) Christmassy films you have ever seen are in fact *films*, starring idle and grossly over-paid actors.

(b) Those blinding and mouth-watering photos of the 'perfect' Christmas table/tree/mantelpiece that have been littering the magazines for weeks – each has taken hours if not days to set up and all of it's *fake*. The turkey is glistening golden brown with the aid of two coats of mahogany Ronseal; the Christmas pudding is dripping with Dulux brilliant white solid emulsion; those perfect shimmering and castellated jellies have been fashioned from acrylic. Not so tasty after all. And all the multimillionaire TV cooks who've been grinningly explaining how to do it 'perfectly'? *They* don't do it at all. They're multi-millionaires, right? They spend Christmas in Barbados.

(c) A 'perfect' wife is a Stepford Wife. Think about it.

3 It would be foolish to tell you to *relax* at this point, but do, for God's sake, try to stop worrying: it's going to be fine. *More* than fine.

4 Pop out and check on the cooking *only if you really have to*. No one needs a jack-in-the-box.

5 Drink the Champagne. It doesn't matter that it's early. Look at you: you need a stiffener. Drink the Champagne.

DING-DONG!

(Or, conceivably:)

BRRR-ING!

No mistaking it that time: it's the doorbell.

Now, I am assuming that you are not cursed with the sort of neighbours who imagine that to pop round unannounced on Christmas morning bearing homemade shortbread is a friendly and festive thing to do (the childless ones, obviously). If you do find yourself prey to this affliction, it is best to lie well in advance. The children all have come down with a virulent and thoroughly debilitating disease. Leprosy is a good one – or, if you feel that might be going it just a bit, then, conceivably, lupus.

Much more likely, though, that the people at the door are in fact the…

RELATIVES

Right, then: a gulp more Champagne. Then you take a deep breath and swing open the door. Hoping earnestly that no mother or aunt or female-in-law has, oh God, *brought their own food*. And that no father or uncle or male-in-law will:

(a) get into politics,

(b) drink too much,

(c) settle down to farting saxophonically.

Or, of course, they may all be positively charming; in the case of family, you play the cards you're dealt. Whatever form the relatives assume, however, you may rest assured that the children will swoop upon them with unfeigned enthusiasm – for while it is true that hairy-faced old men (or women) might well require a hug and a *kiss* (oh *yuk*!) there is, on the other hand, the all-consoling certainty that these ancient peoples from a distant planet will at least have landed laden with *presents*.

And so while the children gabble out their pleasantries ('Hello, Grandad! Hello, Auntie!') – as they cope as best they may with the swooping manifestations of affection – there is really only one thing drumming in their minds. It goes (to the rhythm of a steam train) something like this:

What-have-you-*got*-for-me-what-have-you-*got*-for-me?

What-have-you-*got*-for-me-what-have-you-*got*-for-me?

So let us, on behalf of the oldies, hope that whatever they've got, they've got it right, because following the endless business of hanging up coats, the upping of the central heating thermostat, the passing around of drinkies (not to say that sectioned hostess-plate brimming with assorted nuts which, in common with all other years, will be ritually spurned) it is surely time to start opening the...

PRESENTS

Now if the guidelines laid out earlier in this book have been thoroughly adhered to (unlikely), then all will be well. Otherwise, diplomacy is called for – this, needless to say, being an alien concept so far as all children and very many men are concerned, so once again it might be up to the Woman of the House to steer things gently.

A few pointers:

1 If yours is the sort of family where each member receives just the one gift, then now is the time to tear in generally.

2 If, however, despite your best efforts and that JOKE of a budget, you have overdone it *again* this year, then the process of staggering is the order of the day: one or two now, the rest later on.

3 Beforehand, it might have been a good idea to have instilled into the children the following:

Should they happen upon a gift that disappoints them (too young, too advanced, too last-year's-model, too just, like – *sick*, you know?) they should NOT:

(a) Say 'Oh,' and pretty much wrap it up again.

(b) Whine in a wounded tone, 'Is this supposed to be some sort of a *joke*?'

(c) Burst into tears and run out of the room, slamming the door behind them.

Note: If the Woman of the House is herself let down by a gift, she in turn should NOT:

(a) Say, 'Yes, well – I daresay it's very warm.'

(b) Sniff the unopened package once, lay it aside and say, 'Yes, well.'

(c) Say, 'Yes, well… I do hope you kept the receipt.'

Whatever the Man of the House receives, however – no matter what he might feel – what he must say is:

'Very nice. Thank you.'

And that's that: sorted.

Old people, of course, are never going to like their presents: this is a given. But even so, they really shouldn't say:

(a) 'Well, what does it matter? I'm old.'

(b) 'Yes I can see how you could well have thought I might have liked that:'

(c) 'What do you want to go wasting your money on me for? I'm old.'

'I'm a little cushion
stuffed with lavender.
What are you?'

'Scented bath salts.'

'Aftershave.'

MANNERS IN GENERAL

If you are given...

✳ an item of clothing: try it on immediately. Not underwear, obviously. And not socks.

✳ a book: glance at the blurb, flick through it a bit and say, 'Yes – I look forward to that.'

✳ something to eat or a bottle: say, 'Yum yum. We can all tuck into this little lot, later.'

✳ quality jewellery: say, '*Darling*!' and leave it at that.

✳ costume jewellery: say, 'How pretty! I can think of a few things that will go with.'

✳ a CD: say, 'Ah – my favourite'. Even if it isn't. Or if it really is, but you've already bought it.

CHRISTMAS LUNCH

Now: following this orgy of present-ripping, it is time for the Woman of the House to retire to the kitchen and get serious.

Meanwhile, there is always someone who is genetically programmed to wade through the sea of tattered wrappings and crush it all into a bin bag – this person often contending with someone else (usually much older) who feels equally compelled to carefully smooth out all the larger pieces of paper, peel off the Sellotape, maybe unknot all the ribbons and certainly stow away the pom-pom bows.

Well, leave them to it. It's cooking time now.

But first: have you attended to the table? Ideally, of course, there would exist in the household a time-honoured *tradition* that someone else sees to all that side of things (not too likely, though, is it?). So if it hasn't been done, now is very much the time.

A separate dining room helps, of course. This way, you can get on in peace, knowing that there is to come the added kick of the full revelation when everyone troops in on your word of command. People are always very appreciative of the festive table – not least because Christmas lunch always tends to be a good deal later than everyone anticipated (despite all the timings and plans), by which time people will even have stooped so low as to resort to the assorted nuts and are by now heartily sick of even so much as the sight of the things (and particularly those curled up, dirty-looking wrinkled ones that look like little brains).

So...

The table
What we are aiming at here is a fairly jolly cloth (though not so jolly that it's plastered with robins or the legend 'Ho, Ho, Ho!' picked out in gold thread) and some sort of centrepiece that you didn't use last time (and the time before, and the time before...)

involving as many candles as you can decently cram into it without:

(a) rendering sight of and communication with all other diners as near impossible as makes no difference,

(b) risking heatstroke or conflagration.

Silver always adds a twinkle – but don't, for God's sake, choose this moment to heave down the dusty old canteen and start sliding the tissue off the forks and knives because look: they'll be *tarnished*, won't they? Stainless steel twinkles, too, don't forget, so slam shut the lid and ram the whole lot back again.

Now you have to lay out the crackers, which are all-important. Whatever they may say, everyone likes a cracker. They might feign disdain. They might groan, Oh God – Bloody Little Screwdrivers Again! They might wonder loudly Who Is It Exactly That Actually Uses Miniature Playing Cards? They might gaze dazedly at nail clippers, or a tiny padlock – but rest assured, when a pretty chromium bracelet tumbles out, or a conical bottle stopper, or cuff links, or an If-You-Squint-It-Looks-Just-Like-A-Montblanc biro – then people will quietly pocket their treasure, and set about with gusto reading out the awful gags and riddles.

Also, the tugging and snap and even the eventual litter very much add to the scene – partially, of course, because crackers are still just about the only things that are solely identified with Christmas. Waitrose, John Lewis and Marks & Spencer are best for value; Harrods and Selfridges for (expensive) glamour.

A postscript on crackers
If the children are very young, then get loads of the cheapest crackers possible with the nastiest little plastic contents – they will love them. But whatever crackers you go for, there is one unshakeable rule: everyone has to wear their...

SILLY PAPER PARTY HATS.
Obviously.

Now, then – the lunch itself

Throughout this endeavour, what you must do is *make it easy on yourself*. Or as easy as possible, anyway. The first course will be a ready-made: smoked salmon (dry, wild and excellent and plenty of it – not gloopy-wet, farmed and covered in white stripes and eked out thinly) with maybe some lobster claws and thin brown bread. Or possibly *prosciutto* (try it with pear or peach instead of melon, and just a dusting of fresh ground black pepper).

Puddings, too, will take care of themselves. The *actual* Christmas pudding (get a really good one; Fortnum & Mason still reigns supreme – but don't, needless to say, actually *make* the thing) will be simmering; fresh fruit will have been prepared; a mince pie and maybe a flan and possibly a jelly will certainly take up all the slack (Haagen-Dazs and double cream filling in all the gaps). The jar of Stilton you stick under a lamp for a bit.

You are now free to concentrate on the Main Event. If you have plumped for a goose, you will all morning have been drawing off the fat – to the point where you feel quite ill – and still there is enough of it pouring out of the bloody thing to ensure that the children go 'Oh, *yuk*' at the very sight of it. Better, then, to go for good old turkey, which by now will be golden and gorgeous and filling the house with a real and yummy Christmassy smell. Get help with heaving it out of the oven, because it is a strange truth that if the thing seems heavy when you cram it in, by the time it's cooked, it has all the bulk and dead weight of a defeated Sumo. This perception is due also to the fact that by now you are more than slightly wilting, your body temperature on a par with an oast house.

Now. As you attend to picking out all the golden roasties from the pan and piling high the sprouts (which people do quite like, actually, if they are served *al dente*, with maybe a hollandaise sauce) and filtering the gravy and spooning out the cranberry and divvying up the stuffing and breaking the crispy bacon and chasing around those slippery little chipolatas, it well behoves the Man of the House at this point to carve.

At least in theory. In practice – unless the Man of the House is one of those insufferables who sees the act of carving, like barbecuing, as some noble throwback to Man the Hunter and Gatherer (in which case, prepare to applaud at length) – it is better done in the kitchen by the cook, whenever she can get around to do it. If not, the put-upon Man of the House will:

1 Demand to know where the *proper* fork is.

2 Plaintively enquire how on earth he can be expected to carve with *this* bloody thing – Christ Almighty, it wouldn't cut *butter*…!

3 Squirt his shirt.

4 Take forever.

What he must attend to, however, is every single aspect of…

DRINK

What you need is:

1 Claret. The best you can afford. You don't much taste it, in truth – what with the stuffing and the cranberry and all – but that's not really the point. It's Christmas lunch, so what you need is claret. Latour, in a perfect world.

2 A decent white, for those who think red too 'heavy', or slavishly believe it to be more suitable for poultry. Chablis or Pouilly-Fumé are your best bets here.

3 Beer, fruit juice and mineral water (both the calm and troubled varieties) for those who just frankly don't understand.

4 More Champagne for those who have decided to 'stick' (because it's easy to get the taste, as we all know).

Now: the hostess should finally be seated (having taken off the apron) and she is in need of applause. Eat a bit first – but do not wait for her to anxiously enquire *is everything all right?*

Before this juncture arises (after which all you can offer is weak reassurance) the man should say:

'Excellent, darling. Well-done. Delicious.'

Or another variation on the theme.

At this point, one child will say:
'I said I only wanted the *white* stuff. Don't like the *dark* stuff. It's yuk.'

Another child will say:
'Can we pull the crackers now?'

And an oldie will say:
'It's funny, isn't it? How turkey just doesn't seem to *taste* of anything any more – not like it used to, it doesn't.'

In response to all of which, the Woman of the House will smile like a saint, and feel quite pleased and relieved: another traditional Christmas lunch is well under way.

And all too soon – when the last wodge of Stilton has been piled atop a water biscuit (which will instantly disintegrate); when the last chocolate mint has been ignored by all and then suddenly dived at; when the last oldie has sighed, 'It was good, I'm not saying that, but I think I overdid it…'; when the final demitasse has been slopped all over the cloth; as two of the candles are hastily extinguished because they were dripping quite badly; when the Man of the House extracts a Havana, catches the expression of white-boned terror from a female oldie and the curt and tight-lipped shake of the head from the Woman of the House (and puts the bloody thing away again)…

… now, at last, you know that the time has come for the hallowed and mighty:

'*Santé!*'

Post-Christmas lunch slump

And this is OK. It's important to slump, but only up to a point. Torpor is out – and so is falling asleep on the sofa. Little chance of that with children around, of course, because round about now they – perversely – tend to go into overdrive, prior to later becoming quite cranky (there won't *necessarily* be tears before bedtime, but the possibility is always lurking). There are certain things now that you really ought to approach with care.

Television is not a great idea
You've seen all those old films how many times, anyway? And if the TV is on and people are jabbering, it will annoy in equal measures both those who want it and those who don't. If there's something new and good on, tape it.

The exception to this has to be, of course, the Queen's Christmas message. To some of the older oldies, this *is* Christmas and therefore not to be missed on any account.

'I'd love to watch the Queen, dear,
but she has domestic help.'

Children will moan; tell them it doesn't last long. It is permissible to audibly admire the bouquet of flowers to the side of the Queen. It is usual to speculate upon whether, for her as well as for you, this 'annus' has proved to be more or less 'horribilis' than the last. And it is absolutely *de rigueur* to comment approvingly upon the fact that she smiles more, these days, and that her delivery has grown a good deal less nasal. It is usual to conclude that despite all her money, you wouldn't have her job for all the tea in China.

Board games

Oh, dear. Monopoly will, of course, be rejected because there are far too many people and it takes an age to set up and someone may always be relied upon to get upset if they land on the hotels and anyway it never bloody *ends*. Scrabble is out (too brainy) and that tends to leave things like Trivial Pursuit. But: the oldies will not understand the rules, nor be able to read the cards – and further, they will move their counters any which way but right. The children will be marginalized and bored to stupefaction – and the Man and Woman of the House know the answers to every damn question backwards because they never got around to updating the original set-up, and one of the answers has the President of the United States down as George Bush. Senior.

Old photograph albums
The oldies will at first be absorbed – but this will inevitably lead to:

(a) anecdotes. Yes – all *those* ones. Again.

(b) squirming and shamed embarrassment on the part of the children, when it is recalled how one of them shouted out 'Poo!' at assembly and the other took this as an absolute instruction, and promptly complied.

(c) tears and introspection at the sight of lost but never forgotten sweet old faces and evocative locations.

Charades

The oldies will be unwilling to stand up (or, indeed, unable) and quite rightly do not care for being seen to make absolute bloody fools of themselves. The children will, no matter what you say, blurt out words, and acrimony is sure to result in the form of muttered bewilderment and scorn, on the lines of 'How was standing on one leg and pulling at your eyelids supposed to be Audrey *Hepburn*, for Christ's sake?!'

So, better by far just to let the afternoon drift. There are new toys to be explored (once they've been put together and batteried up). There is drink to be drunk, choccies to be gorged and – a bit later on, something of a highlight: not just turkey sandwiches, but *a nice cup of tea*, which the oldies will tell you

(a) they have been gasping for, but didn't like to ask

(b) they could well have done with at lunch, but didn't like to ask

(But nonetheless – when it arrives it will be roundly deemed: Too Weak. And the lady who commented on the tasteless turkeys of today will be moved to wonder why it is that nobody any longer seems to know how to make a good strong cup of tea; does anyone even *use* a pot? Let alone warm it?)

THE MAN OF THE HOUSE, at this point, is generally quite content (and why, the Woman of the House, might archly enquire, bloody shouldn't he be?) A few things might arise, however, to cast a shadow:

1 The fact that he's not allowed to smoke this sodding cigar. It's not that he's a martyr to it – it's just that in the past years, before the Nazi Anti-Smoking Lobby took the world by its throat, everyone used to say how lovely and Christmassy the *smell* was. Mm. But mainly – it's because he's not allowed to. And this inhibition can in turn lead to the first hint of feeling just a bit

STIR CRAZY.

Could he, maybe, slope off for a bit? Just slip out for a little while, could he? But there's nowhere to *go*, is there? Maybe just the garden (to smoke the sodding cigar)? No – too damned cold. Christ.

2 The lowering knowledge (remember two Christmases ago?) that if anything can go wrong in the house (the boiler, the fuses). then this is round about the moment it will pick. And what do you do if it does? Call out some cowboy at £100 a minute? Freeze? Stumble about in the dark? (Remember two Christmases ago? Had to take all four batteries out of the just-unwrapped Action Man tank just to get the bloody torch to work – which did not go down well with a certain party.)

And yes, OK: nothing's happened *yet*, granted. But what if it does? Down to the Man of the House, isn't it? But could he cope? Because he does, at this moment, feel, if he's being perfectly honest, just the teeniest bit sandbagged (which comes as a blessed relief). So what he thinks he'll do is pour another drink...

...and settle back in the armchair and survey the scene.

It is, in truth, a good and mellow scene. Everything is warm and messy, just like last year. Everyone appears to be spoiled and stuffed and generally enjoying themselves, after their respective fashions. The oldies chatting and nibbling and dozy; the children still diverted, thank the Lord. The Woman of the House finally getting to enjoy her *well-earned rest*.

And still perched foolishly atop her head – whether she is aware of it or not – is her silly paper party hat.

Bless.

But listen: here's a thought. Of the twelve days of Christmas this is just the *first*...

3

now we must enter…
the twilight zone

BOXING DAY, really, can be anything you want it to be. For some, it forms merely a continuation of the day before: more television, more turkey sandwiches, a good deal more slumping, and certainly a lot more drink. Others either host or go to afternoon parties. On the whole, however, these tend not to be a good idea because:

(a) If you are to be a host, you have to clean up the house.

(b) If you are to be a guest, you have to clean up yourself.

(c) If you are desperately hungover, you have to clean up your act.

Others are fans of the *good brisk walk*, which, by way of a pick-me-up and a stand-by, they see to be on a par with *the nice cup of tea*, which naturally you will partake of both before and after said *good brisk walk*.

Should you rouse yourself and plump for

this course of action, you will see in parks and on heaths lots of couples and even whole families attired as if for a photograph to go in a mail-order catalogue: Christmas present Rupert scarves, multi-striped mitt 'n' woolly pom-pom hat combos and a good many quilted car coats. Here we have the constitutional as underpinned with mild exhibitionistic overtones.

At some point during (or even instead of) the *good brisk walk*, many will make for the pub, for one of the three reasons:

1 Being seen to savour a pint of foaming ale before a crackling log fire on a frost-kissed and festive morning

2 A pub lunch – because no one can, frankly, face the thought of

(**a**) cooking

(**b**) turkey sandwiches

3 The pursuit of the Hair of the Dog

The only other reason to go out on Boxing Day is to scour the garage shops for a further gross of batteries in order to ensure that all the winking and blooping electronic contrivances can continue to drive you up the wall for the whole of the day, and on into the night.

If, however, you stay at home, then you will find yourself doing at least one, and most likely all, of the following:

1 Idly observing that there are four or five baubles – one of them shattered – at the base of the tree, lying like dead men amid a coating of needles and tangles of lametta. And further idly observing that they can bloody well stay there.

'After today, it's cold turkey on booze, and cold turkey sandwiches...'

2 Eating turkey sandwiches. Or turkey pie. Or turkey hash. Or turkey fricassee. Or else in desperation phoning for a Chinese takeaway and finding that they're not open today. And nor is the Indian.

3 Watching television. You will not concentrate upon the programmes, of course: more old films and manic nonentities who are apparently celebrities fronting an eternal stream of 'Christmas Specials', all of which were recorded last August.

No. The programmes will pass you by. What will impress themselves upon you, however, are
THE ADS.
As they are meant to do. Because they appear to be on a loop – a drip-feed of frantic clamouring that seeps into your veins. The following varieties will seek to become a part of you:

THE SALES

Yes: the high street and the out-of-town superstores are after you again. All the stuff you did not slog around for and shell out big bucks on in the tortured weeks leading up to Christmas they expect you to rush right back for and scoop up now.

With the added inducement, of course, that prices now have been: *slashed*!

You are *not* meant to think:
Christ: everything I bought is still for sale and now the price is *slashed*.

You *are* meant to think:
If I am not quick I shall lose out on the opportunity of a lifetime...
...because these sales start at 9am

TOMORROW!

And the six o'clock news will later show you film of these very wise people indeed who have been camping outside a certain department store since the night before Christmas Eve – and so, while the likes of you have spent their time eating and drinking, keeping warm, enjoying family and presents, these enlightened souls have opted instead for the higher ground. And still they lie cocooned within a duvet on the wet and ice-bound pavement, smug in the certainty that, come the morning of December 27th (should they not have seized up and died in the night), they will secure for themselves

(a) a slap-up breakfast, courtesy of a Page Three girl from a tabloid newspaper;

(b) a giant plasma TV for little more than the price of a packet of fags.

It's the sort of spirit that made this country what it is today. I'm afraid.

And in between these relentless sales ads, you might find yourself wondering:

*Who could actually **bear** the thought of going round the shops again, so very terribly soon?*

*And who, actually, could still **afford** to?*

Sofas

No longer merely an offshoot of the sales in general, but truly now a galaxy, out there on its own. There was, you remember, very energetic action on the sofa front during the run-up to Christmas, largely on the lines of

Order Now at this unrepeatable price and by Christmas you too can be sprawling all over the sofa as long as a boat and flaunting your naked feet and your glass of nice red wine while laughing your bloody head off, just like our smug young models here!

But post-Christmas, they go quite ballistic. As you sit slumped in fully-fledged Boxing Day mode (on your sofa), you will be bombarded with screamingly insistent bulletins concerning the state of the warehouses up and down the country, each of them exploding with more damn sofas than there are human beings on the planet. And the best news they keep till last: the pre-Christmas unrepeatable prices are to be not just repeated but... *slashed!*

And in between these relentless sofa ads, you might find yourself wondering:

*Who **are** all these people in constant need of sofas? What is wrong with the sofa they've **got**?*

*And even if buying a brand-new sofa is an appealing idea, who, actually, could still **afford** to?*

'It's called Boxing Day because all the stupid presents go back in their boxes for someone else next year...'

Holidays

Endless white-gold sandy beaches and some seductive panning shots of thatch-roofed bars which some mad fool has dumped in the sea so that you have to wade in waist deep whenever you feel in need of a belt. A nut-brown and Ambre Solaire sweet-and-sticky bikini-clad beauty, lolling on a hammock strung between palm trees, the drinking straws in her rainbow cocktail kissing at her pouty-fat and pinky lips. It would be foolish to deny that, all in all, there is *something to be said for it*.

But nonetheless, in between these relentless holiday ads, you might find yourself wondering: who is it – cast adrift amid the exhausting lassitude of a Boxing Day slump – who can actually get their minds around

   (a) embarking on an early morning blitz on the high-street sales,

   (b) planning a drive out to the suburban sofa superstore,

   (c) booking a fortnight in Paradise for half a year away?

(And who, actually, could still *afford* to?)

Such reservations on your part might well be accompanied by...

THE VERY FIRST STIRRINGS OF UNEASE
...as you begin to realize just how much you must have chalked up to your credit cards during the endless Christmas approach. And whatever the sum that's nagging you, you may be sure that the true total figure is far higher than that. Because:

(a) You're trying to be kind to you

(b) You can't quite bring yourself to face the awful truth

(c) It's weeks since you gave up any attempt at keeping track

So you may feel very much in two minds as the next wash of ads floods into your being – because these are wholly concerned with impressing upon you with sonorous urgency not just the consummate ease of obtaining loans but also the way in which said loans can at a single stroke *reduce your monthly outgoings.*

This phenomenon is called, rather sweetly, consolidation. But: you are surely not so swaddled by an insistent indolence and a slick of booze that you can fail to realize that loans cost money; it's as simple as that. Close on thirty percent, a lot of them.

And so, no matter how tempting or attractive it may appear to take up these nice gentlemen on their offer of loans in the light of the pre-Christmas blow-out and the high street sales – which you'll probably look in on – and the almost inevitable purchase of at least one of those sofas and the booking of a frankly necessary fortnight in Paradise, you might find yourself wondering…

WHO COULD ACTUALLY AFFORD TO?

Boxing Day (although it rarely seems it) will eventually pass. And in the old days, of course, *that was it*. All over for another year: pack away all the nonsenses and get back to work. Things are different, now – largely because for so many years the thinking of the average working man and woman has gone something like this:

*Monday and Tuesday are **official** holidays, right? So it follows that I'll take the Wednesday as well and so I'll probably feel like utter hell come Thursday – so tend to give **that** a miss, I think – and who the hell is going to go in on a Friday? Mug's game, right? And so then comes the weekend (thank God: about time) and then it's pretty much New Year, isn't it? Which, as we all know, can take a while to get over…*

And so, officially or otherwise, every single day between Christmas Eve and New Year's Day (inclusive) has become *holiday time*. This is a minimum of ten days, and can often be more. A long time. And let's face it, for people not really used to being at home much at all, all this can be an absolute *nightmare*.

Which is why, at this time of year, an envious glance is cast in the direction of the likes of

(a) journalists
(b) doctors and nurses
(c) taxi drivers

...and even, God help us, the people who try to sell us not just holidays and sofas, but also loans. Anyone, in short, who has a damn good reason to be elsewhere. Because by now, elsewhere's looking good. For women, the pressure of cooking and vastly increased housework and ceaseless responsibility and cooking and keeping the children constantly entertained and forever clearing up after everybody and cooking and never having so much as a moment to herself and bloody *cooking* is by now rather evidently beginning to tell.

While for the man, the constant pressure of noise and lots of people and hoovering and lack of privacy and washing machines and children and the lack of destination or point or direction or even some small vestige of *hope* is by now rather evidently beginning to tell.

'Who gave you the
idea we only go
out once a year?'

Because, after all the razzmatazz, there now comes the letdown. And too much time in which to let it sink in. But: the year will not just wither away and die – oh, no. There is a secret weapon up its sleeve, and it does keep a lot of us going, knowing the score. Because, look: if any given year is all but played out... then it surely follows that yet another is in the wings and *looming*.

Indeed.

And here it comes now...

4

raise your glass for...
the last hurrah

HOW YOU ELECT to spend New Year's Eve will wholly depend upon your

(a) age,

(b) remaining levels of optimism,

(c) threshold of pain.

The very young, *of course*, will be out for the whole of the night, and very possibly the following night, too. But right up until around 9pm on New Year's Eve, they will not have a clue as to exactly where or how they are going to spend it. This does not remotely faze them. On the contrary: here is the embodiment of *cool*, because others are to infer that there are very many options open to them, each one no big hassle. It's simply a question of cruising, hanging loose, linking up and (eventually) crashing.

So casual an attitude is seen by older people, of course, to be frankly incomprehensible, if not downright appalling – because naturally they have known for weeks *precisely* where they will be, what they will be doing and (in the case of the women, anyway) exactly what they will be wearing while doing it.

Unless you are very new to the game, it has to be said that all of the options are fairly grim. For what it's worth, then, here they are.

Going to a party with 'friends'
This is rather like drinks with the People-Next-Door-But-One, writ large. There is nothing to do until midnight except drink – which helps maintain the ceaseless and quite manic grin of near-deranged delight which is mandatory for all. It is also *de rigueur* to at all times wear a silly paper party hat, and to burst balloons with cigarette ends and blow through those rolled-up paper hooter things with a feather on the end. Poppers and streamers are also much in evidence.

When midnight strikes, you drink more and repeat all of the above, but with added zip and whooping. You must also join hands with a fair few drunken strangers, and if you're not very careful you will, at this juncture, be kissed or even groped. This is called celebration.

Though after you have done with ringing out the 'old', you might find yourself observing with a crushing sense of doom, that the freshly rung in 'new' seems somehow sneakily familiar. At such a point you must try not to be sick either literally or metaphysically. And (more important) to keep a good distance from anyone who has come to look a little greenish, or whose cheeks have ballooned and by their eyes you can tell are worried. The thing to do now is either leave with miserable-as-sin designated driver, or courtesy of a ruinously expensive minicab. Or else continue to drink till dawn or insensibility, whichever is the first to overtake you.

*'It's Malcolm.
What are we
doing for New
Year's Eve?'*

Throwing a party for 'friends'

This follows the lines of the foregoing option, with the added bonus of devastated carpets, colossal expenditure, and so much clearing up to face the following afternoon (or whenever) that you will come very close to weeping, if not tip right over the edge altogether, and shamelessly sob your heart out.

Going to a restaurant or hotel for dinner, with or without 'friends'

Which is fine...

...*if* you are happy to part with hundreds of pounds per head for a perfectly modest supper, be nauseated by the waiters' over-familiarity, and somehow fetch up home at 4am in a laughably expensive taxi, in order to relieve the hysterically expensive baby-sitter.

'I can't remember the
last time I heard you
go "Ho! Ho! Ho!"'

Trudging off in the freezing dark to somewhere that is rumoured to have a spectacular display of fireworks at the stroke of midnight

You must resign yourself to hanging about and making gigglingly inane small talk with perfect strangers for hours and hours while stamping your feet in an effort to keep the circulation flowing. At the first bong of the midnight bell, dumbly witness the fizz and sparkle of a selection of squibs. Allow four times the length of time it took you to reach there in order to get home.

Staying in, with anyone who agrees that here is the wisest course

Sit there, waiting for midnight, feeling quite foolish. Watch far too much profoundly embarrassing television. Drink Champagne at midnight, having stupidly clinked glasses. Note that it gives you wind. Go to bed.

If you plump for this final option, then it is unlikely that the following morning you will be suffering from

A HANGOVER
All the other scenarios, of course, virtually guarantee it.

So how do you go about treating this tenderly fragile state of yours? What do you do if you feel that all you want to do is

(a) wait for death,

(b) not wait for death, but kill yourself *now?*

It sometimes helps to analyze precisely just how bad you are feeling, and exactly which of your parts is giving you grief. Here, then, are the usual suspects...

'Get me another
sherry, dear.'

1 If you feel that the Boxer Rebellion is re-enacting itself deep within the pit of your stomach, it might help to eat something nondescript and friendly: bread (not toast – too spiky) or – if you can face the gloopy sight of it – porridge. I *know* they say a fry-up is the thing, but they're wrong, aren't they?

2 If you feel that your palate and tongue – despite much clacking – are as arid as a drugget in the tundra, then gallons and gallons of water are the thing. And of course you should have glugged it down before you went to sleep – but, naturally, you didn't. So do it now.

3 If you feel that your head has been bound up tight in Duck Tape by some cackling joker at some point during your fevered coma, and that your eyes are like hard little chestnuts rolling around on a vendor's brazier – then the cold compress, the darkened room and the regular paracetamol is the cure for you. That, of course, and time.

4 If you feel on the whole pretty much OK, rather surprisingly – just a bit shaky and maybe a bit cold, but all in all not too bad – then the hair of the dog will put you to rights in no time: a well-made Bloody Mary, say. Of course, when this wears off you'll be back where you started – so best just sit it out. Soon, you'll be fine.

And as to avoiding the hangover altogether, here is the one and only truth: there are only two ways:

(a) Don't drink.

(b) Don't stop.

In Scotland, of course, escaping a hangover is simply not an option. Christmas over the border is seen to be no more, really, than a dry run, a foretaste of the real thing to come...

HOGMANAY

...during which you must cope with the quaint etiquette of

FIRST-FOOTING

...whereby at the sound of pealing bells on the stroke of midnight on December 31st, you must present yourself at someone's front door in order to be the first over the threshold in the new year. It helps if you are tall and dark; handsome is optional, but always welcome.

In addition, you must have about you:
   (**a**) a bottle of whisky (preferably single malt),
   (**b**) shortbread,
   (**c**) a lump of coal. Obviously.
   (**d**) at least a modicum of sobriety (the night is young).

It is more of an honour to 'first-foot' than to be 'first-footed', so often after midnight no one's at home to be visited. Would-be first-

'Where in God's name
have you been?'

footers therefore amble on (at least with whisky and shortbread to sustain them, if needs be; and to hell with the coal, quite frankly).

In most places – and especially Edinburgh, *the* place to be – partying in the streets continues through the night. The kilt is often worn – and with especial enthusiasm by English and American visitors who have no damn right to.

On New Year's Day it is traditional to have a late lunch (or early high tea) with all the extended family, throughout which crippling hangovers are manfully dealt with and Scottish songs are sung and poets like Burns (well, actually, *only* Burns) are recited and no irony whatever is, for a moment, detectable.

So anyway. Here we are with a brand...

NEW YEAR

And although, strictly speaking, January 2nd ought, by rights, to be a regular working day, it isn't, of course. So there is still more time to fill. And though you very probably have not made any formal New Year resolutions, it is possible nonetheless that your mind – maybe fuelled by the great January raft of dumb and predictable articles in all of the papers ('Getting Back Into Shape!') – might well be edging you towards considering a purge.

Partly Puritan guilt, of course. After all this self-indulgence, there must inevitably follow a price to pay (and preferably one where deprivation and pain are well to the fore). Such an inclination might also be prompted by the fact that you find yourself these days pouring a pre-lunch stiffener as a matter of course... or maybe because you can't do up your waistband... or conceivably you are getting this mildly worrying ache on one side (it's not a *pain*, exactly...).

If any of these apply, you might begin to toss around the possibility of opting for one of the following.

The gym

You could well be a member of a health club. You might not have been there since the day you signed on. You might think that now would be as good a time as any to get your money's worth. The most likely outcome of all this musing is that you will simply continue to muse. Or – who knows? – you might actually get yourself down there (check it out). If so, you will find the following:

(a) dauntingly toned and fit people, younger and far lovelier than you;

(b) dauntingly toned and fit people, older and far lovelier than you;

(c) a basic exercise machine sneeringly set for you at Level One that whips you up into a lather, leaving you crying openly and utterly spent.

'This is where those yoga classes pay off...'

The detox

This process used to be called 'going on a diet' and/or 'giving up the booze'. But *detox*, well: it sounds like a *system*, doesn't it? It has the ring of a *regime*. And the concept is, admittedly, a pleasing one: ridding the body of all those noxious things – what can be the downside?

At first, it might even come as a *relief*. Who, in January, honestly desires Christmas pudding and Drambuie Cream Liqueur? And some people quite ritually go the whole month of January without alcohol (there are no parties – fewer temptations generally), and if you can survive the paralyzing boredom of sparkling water and orange juice, very good luck to you.

But if you *do* manage to eschew the drink and all tasty things, know this: *you'll be back*. It's simply a matter of when. You might manage the whole month; or you could pitch off the wagon on the morning of Day One.

That said, there exists a very fashionable method of prolonging the dream. It is called a

Twelve-step programme

These programmes (which always, somewhat suspiciously, have twelve steps exactly – no more and no less) are tailored to not just people addicted to alcohol: oh, no. There are programmes for Debtaholics (maybe worth thinking about, at this time of year) as well as Sexaholics, Rageaholics, Wheataholics and Chocoholics. You might try one. It could just hit your button.

If, however, you remain committed to the principle of Detox, the basic rules are these:

IN: mineral water. Gallons and gallons of it. And herbal tea. Gallons and gallons of it.
OUT: caffeine, alcohol, bread, red meat, sugar, chocolate

I know this seems to tot up to the ingredients for just one damn good meal, but what are you supposed to do? The purest detox should really be contemplated only by those with ultra-light duties and an awful lot of time. Most of which, by the way, will be spent in the lavatory.

The health check-up

This, needless to say, needs to be done privately – not least because otherwise you might have to wait so long for an appointment that you could, during the interim, die of old age. And rest assured: it is all conducted in the best possible taste largely by a briskly efficient beige and inoffensive nurse in a similarly beige and inoffensive clinic. You go there, at the appointed hour – having eaten and drunk nothing whatever for the requisite six hours, as instructed – and all you feel (apart from parched and ravenous) is a mounting sense of *dread*, not to say naked fear. Because in theory, anyway, you are stumping up a fair slice of cash in order to find out whether anything notable is wrong with you, right? Right. It's just that *you don't want to know.*

But look: you're here now, so you might as well get on with it. You come armed with your filled-in health questionnaire – throughout which you will have lied, but not too brazenly. Such dishonesty is wholly advisable, by the way, because the doctors routinely half or double anything you write, and always to your detriment.

You also have with you unspeakable samples, and now you are required to contribute more, albeit of a different nature. Blood is one of them. They tell you will feel a little prick – which you have been doing, if you're honest, since the moment you walked through the door. You will be weighed (and you will be convinced their equipment is faulty).

There are separate and quite different humiliations lined up for both men and women, to be sure that no one escapes. Your strength, hearing, eyesight and body-fat ratio will all assessed (and you will be convinced their equipment is faulty). And then a doctor – a total stranger to you – will ask if you want to discuss with him or her the most intimate fears and truths concerning your entire life and history on earth, and to this generous invitation you will answer 'No'.

Not that you are really listening, in truth. Because what you are filled with still is a mounting sense of dread because now you're going to be told what's what. Don't worry. In the vast majority of cases, everything comes out fine.

Because if you *are* a bit overweight, or short-sighted or hard of hearing (*did you get that?*) – well. You already *knew*, didn't you? The chances of anything nasty being thrown up are extremely remote (which, perversely, fails to thrill you: you merely remain convinced that their equipment is faulty).

The declutter programme

Under this seemingly innocuous umbrella title, there lie skulking three quite different areas of concern:

(**a**) stuff,

(**b**) partner,

(**c**) job.

We will deal with them one by one.

STUFF is quite easy. The truth that you are drowning amid a sea of gathered belongings might occur to you when you have taken down all the Christmas decorations (which you are well advised to see to, incidentally, no later than the 2nd of January; waiting for the twelfth day of Christmas is merely prolonging the agony. Listen: the tree looks a wreck, Christmas is *over* – get rid of it all, for God's sake). So suddenly, the room seems less fussy and so much clearer – so why not extend this new feeling of space and heave out more *stuff*?

I'll tell you why: because someone else will object. And if they counter-suggest some alternative stuff to chuck out... well, then *you* will object. This is basically why so much clutter has accumulated in the first place.

The PARTNER thing is altogether more serious. As has been said, this is the time of year when couples are forced together for much longer than usual, with little respite – and this is good news for divorce lawyers everywhere. Relationships can let people down in so many ways, though, at this red-raw and chilly time.

So you think you want a new JOB? Or is it that you simply cannot face going back to the old one? Change for change's sake is not always a good thing, you know. But if it really *is* time for a fresh start – then know this:

1 Answering an ad in a paper need not be so hopeless as you might imagine. Many do not apply because they (like you) assume that *everyone* will. If there is an application form, so much the better. They are a turn-off for most people. But not for you.

2 Recruitment companies are maybe not ideal. They each receive hundreds of CVs per day (and more in the New Year) and yours is just one of them, languishing there.

3 Try to be headhunted. Bit of a Catch-22, though. If you are truly headhuntable, it will have happened by now.

4 The direct approach is best. Don't write to 'Personnel' or 'Human Resources'. Go straight to the top banana. Make it clear that you know about and applaud his company, and lay out succinctly how your presence could make it even better.

All this chasing new work, though (it has to be said) is a damn lot of *work*. Which is why most people eventually stay put. It's maybe wise. Giving up *any* job, these days, may be seen to be rather rash. You'll get through.

Because look at it this way: you've just survived CHRISTMAS, haven't you? Even rather enjoyed it. Well, then: you can now face anything else the world has to throw at you.

HAPPY NEW YEAR.

Or, to put it another way:
HERE WE GO AGAIN.